ST. SIMONS ISLAND

ENCHANTING GOLDEN ISLE

ST. SIMONS ISLAND

ENCHANTING GOLDEN ISLE

PHOTOGRAPHY BY BERT THOMPSON
TEXT BY GLENDA COCHRAN

Dunes, East Beach

Published by Island House Publishing Company, Inc.
P.O. 6975, Macon, Georgia 31208, (912) 743-5689

Library of Congress Catalog Number: 88-061427
ISBN: 0-940379-01-5
Manufactured in the United States of America

First Edition

Edited by Glenda Cochran
Designed by Becky Holcombe
Typography by Carole Barker
Illustration by Marcia Wetzel
Printed by Kingsport Press, Inc.

For Barbara and Bill Thompson,
my parents.

Bert Thompson

In memory of my Grandfather,
Johnnie Calvin Scurry (1893-1988),
a man who loved St. Simons Island.

Glenda Cochran

FOREWORD

There is a mystical sense about St. Simons Island that is enchanting. Here, surrounded by vast fields of watery marsh and the sea, there is a feeling of being outside reality, buffered from pressures and demands, as if removed from the confines of time.

Like a wonderland, the island seems magical. Its beauty is mesmerizing. Its past is enthralling. Its ambience is lighthearted and fun. And above all, it has a mysterious and ellusive charm that is extraordinary and compelling. There are endless ways in which St. Simons delights, but it is with subtlety that the island touches and captivates the heart.

Shrimp boat, St. Simons Sound

Freshwater pond

INTRODUCTION

Few places on earth are as delightfully magical as St. Simons Island, the most historic of Georgia's Golden Isles. Quaint, naturally beautiful, and mysteriously enchanting, it has become one of the most favored resort and residential islands on the South Atlantic Coast. Its charm capitivates young and old alike. It offers fun for the heart, tranquility for the soul, and for the spirit, revitalization.

Lying at the edge of the Atlantic Ocean, about 25 miles north of the Florida line, St. Simons is a mossy link in a chain of nine major barrier islands that parallel Georgia's coast, a fascinating part of one of the world's most unique estuarine systems. The region contains about one-third of all the salt marsh on the eastern coast of the United States (approximately 500,000 acres).

South of St. Simons is Jekyll Island and Georgia's southernmost island, Cumberland. Eastward are Sea Island, Little St. Simons Island, and the Atlantic Ocean. North, beyond a few smaller islands, is Sapelo Island. Westward is Brunswick, Glynn Gounty, Gcorgia, thc island's county seat and nearest mainland port.

A five-mile stretch of highway and bridges connects Brunswick and St. Simons, one of only four Georgia sea islands accessible by car. Before touching the island's southwest shore, this causeway, the F. J. Torras, travels through a vast expanse of meadow marsh, and over several tidal streams, including Terry Creek, Back River, Little River, Mackay River, and the Frederica River. The unique beauty here inspired Sidney Lanier's famous poem, "The Marshes of Glynn."

The island's shores are bluffs and beaches, edged by river, marsh, long broad inlets, and the open sea. Its land area is approximately 12 miles long, north to south, and four miles wide at its broadest point, about the size of Manhatten. Its natural interior is a maritime complex of vine-tangled woodlands, swamps, meadows, and marsh.

Along the island's sandy lanes, black-top roads, and bicycle paths, meticulous landscaping and a picturesque variety of shanties, cottages, traditional homes, opulent estates, country clubs, and luxurious resorts contribute to the ambience. The result is a cozy blend of the modest and elegant, old and new, among a lush profusion of southern zone and semitropical flora.

Especially enchanting are the island's live oak trees. Their massive trunks and lanquid limbs form beautiful canopies just about everywhere on the island. With wispy strands of Spanish moss draping from nearly every bough, these magical trees give the island the look and feel of a wonderland.

Wildlife is abundant in the island habitat. An estimated seventy percent of all commercially important species of fish and shellfish live in the surrounding waters. During their seasons, especially at dawn and dusk, processions of shrimp boats attest to the bounty, as do the numerous birds that forage the beaches and sandbars, and follow the shrimpers' nets. Insects, reptiles, amphibians, rodents, marsupials, and mammals share the environment as well.

St. Simons began to accommodate human inhabitants, American Indians, well over 500 years ago. Since then the island has been the stage for political drama, social upheaval, romance, legend, and myth. Five flags have flown over its shores: French, Spanish, English, Confederate, and the U.S. Even the pirates' "jolly roger" had its sway.

The fort and town of Frederica, built on the island's northwest shore by the English in 1736, became one of the most significant military settlements in colonial American history. Today, it is a national park and shrine. Nearby, another revered landmark, Christ Church, Frederica, is the second oldest Episcopal church in the diocese of Georgia. In its churchyard, which is shaded by extraordinarily majestic oaks, are the gravestones of many of the island's early settlers.

During the years of the antebellum South, cotton fields blanketed the island. St. Simons planters made agricultural history and gained world renown as America's first cultivators of sea island cotton, a long staple, silky white cotton which sold in European markets for more than twice the price of ordinary cotton.

After the island's plantation economy was brought to a close by the Civil War, St. Simons became the center for what grew to be the third largest lumber sawing and shipping operation in the country. Concurrently, the island's appeal as a summer resort began to blossom. No longer a private "cotton island," its accessibility for vacations and retreats ushered in a new era.

Thousands of sojourners have since been charmed by St. Simons' magic. It is said that once the sands of St. Simons have been in your shoes, you are sure to return. The truth in that statement transformed St. Simons from a sparsely populated little paradise into the tourist mecca it is today.

Unlike the island's early inhabitants, modern islanders no longer have to hunt, fish, grow, or go into Brunswick for food and supplies. The island has shopping centers, fashionable shops, quaint boutiques, and an array of restaurants offering culinary feasts, from fast foods to seven-course extravaganzas.

The majority of the island's residential, recreational, and commercial communities are nestled in its southern section along five principal roads and in the oceanside village where the island's pier and lighthouse are landmark attractions. The north end of the island is the least populated, although residential development there is increasing.

The island's current year-round population is approximately 14,000, a figure that is growing and more than doubles during the summer months. Even so, St. Simons has embraced its popularity without relinquishing its charm and serenity. Its pace has remained unhurried and casual – its prevailing atmosphere intimate and remote. It is truly a Golden Isle.

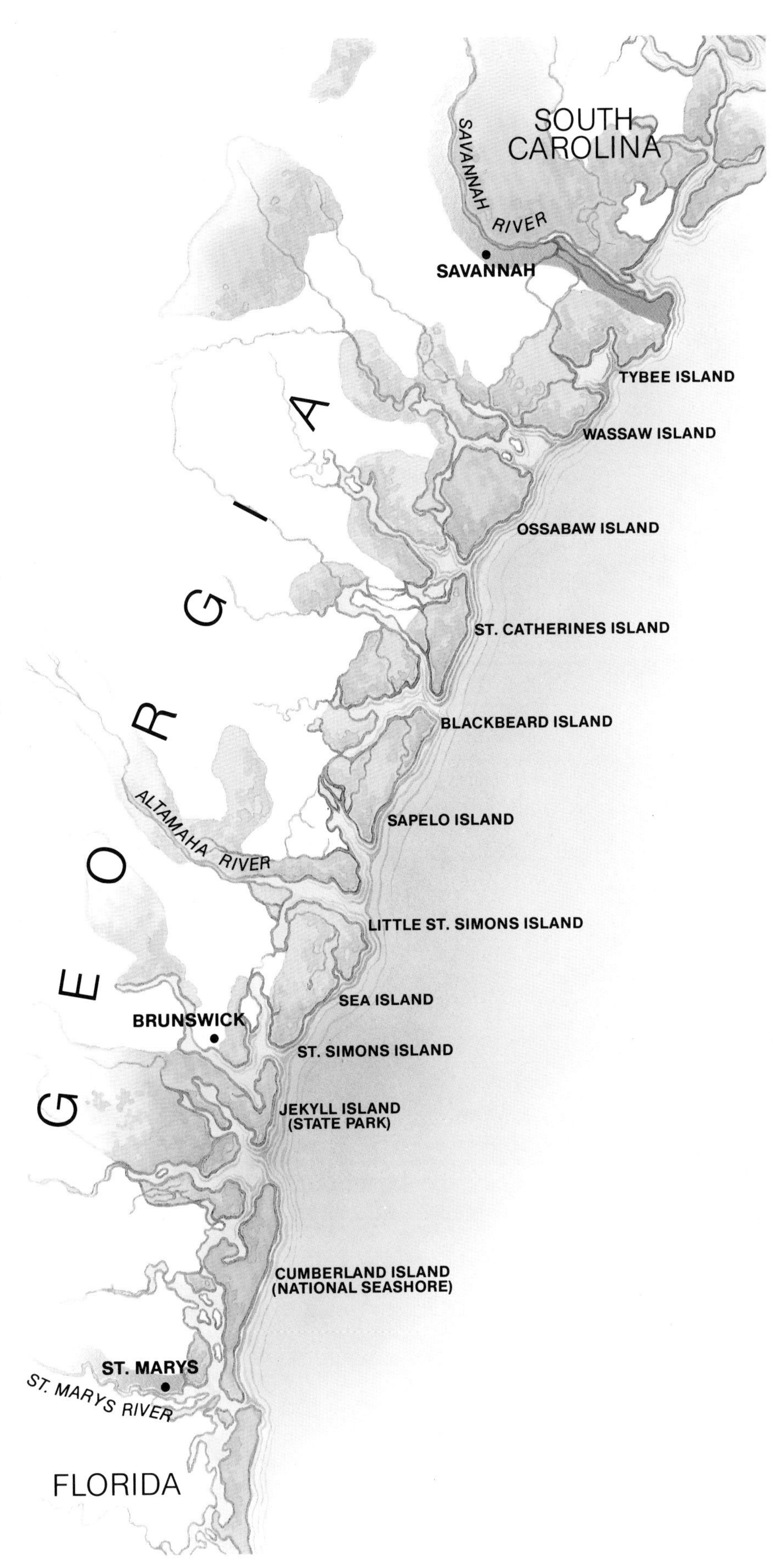

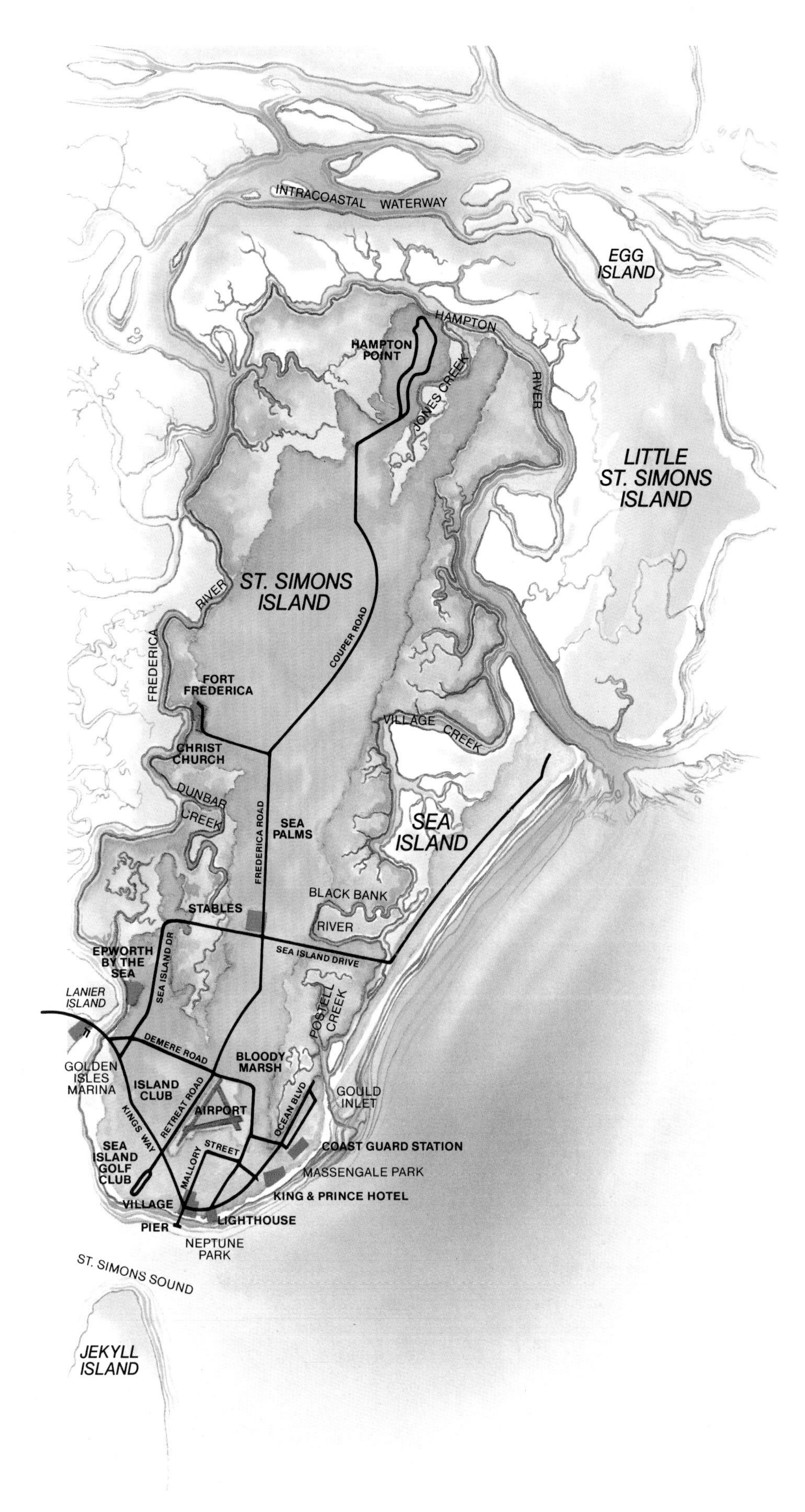

GEOLOGY

Millions of years of geologic process took place before St. Simons and the area we now recognize as Georgia's coast took shape. At one time America's southeastern seaboard was occupied by a much larger island known as Appalachia. This ancient island extended from the Gulf of Mexico to Maryland. As the earth convulsed, Appalachia was supplanted by the continental land we know today.

With the onset of the Ice Ages, Georgia's coastal region continued to change. Because of thermal contractions and expansions of the ocean, the shoreline shifted substantially.

At a high point, the state's coast was as far as 300 miles inland along the Fall Line, the juncture of the Coastal Plain and the Piedmont Plateau. Sand dunes, vestiges of that early shore, can be found near Columbus, Macon, Milledgeville, and Augusta. At a low point, the Atlantic receeded well out into its basin, 80 miles offshore from St. Simons' current location.

As sea levels fluctuated, different sets of barrier islands were created. Some formed as water drained from the mainland, others as the ocean rose. Although they lie in close proximity to one another, and in some cases even merge, there are really two sets of sea islands along the Georgia coast today.

Georgia's westward set of coastal islands, including St. Simons, began to form 35,000 to 40,000 years ago. The Atlantic was receeding then and the sea level was around six feet higher than it is now. Georgia's eastward islands formed about 4,000 to 5,000 years ago during our current Ice Age thaw.

As sea levels rose, the younger islands migrated westward. Some became juxtaposed with the older, more developed islands. Others, like the two that border St. Simons, Little St. Simons and Sea Island, have remained distinct.

ECOLOGY

In its infancy, St. Simons was either a sandbar or a sand dune that withstood the erosive effects of winds, waves, and tidal currents. Over time, it stabilized and lagoons were created on its landward sides. The lagoons eventually filled with riverine sediment and became salt marsh. The island's seaward side continued to be shaped by the surf.

Today, St. Simons is a well-developed composite of ocean beach, salt marsh, maritime forest, and freshwater slough. While sand and salt are common to its terrain, a large portion of the island's soil is rich with humus as much as eight feet deep.

Most of the island's seaward shore is buffered from the Atlantic by the two younger islands, Little St. Simons and Sea Island. South of their protection, St. Simons greets the waves with over two miles of white, sandy beach.

Parallel to the beach flats are the island's sand dune communities. These environments, important barriers against tidal erosion, are extremely fragile. Foot traffic easily destroys them. When the roots of stabilizing plants like sea oats, beach croton, and fiddle-leaf morning glory are disrupted, the sands lose their anchors, and the dunes "blow-out."

In addition to humans, benign visitors such as sand crabs scurry across St. Simons' dunes. Although it is rare, logger-head turtles can be seen among the dunes, too. These huge, barnacle encrusted marine reptiles use sand dunes as landmarks for their annual egg laying missions. A few, guided by St. Simons' dunes, come ashore to dig their cache.

Prickly pears, sand spurs, and shrub zone plants, like wax myrtle, casina (or *yaupon*) holly, and yucca grow behind the dunes where the effects of salt-water spray is less intense. These, along with transition trees, such as red bays, marsh elders, cabbage palms, and saltcedars, are predominant in border communities near the beach and inner-island marshes. These same species are also seen in marsh islands, or hammocks.

Several tidal creeks flow around and within the island's interior. Along their banks are boggy fields of marsh grass. While these areas may seem lifeless, they are deceiving. Constantly energized by the sun and tide, salt marsh is one of the most biologically active cultures on earth. The offspring of various marine species are nurtured here until they grow large enough to survive in the sea. Many land and avian species visit to feed and seek shelter. There are also full-time residents such as marsh hens, fiddler crabs, and snails.

Island ground below sea level is flooded by seven foot tides twice a day. Depending upon relative elevation, and time and depth of tidal inundation, these areas can be classified according to ecological zones, such as levee marsh, low marsh, and high marsh.

Levee marsh, the lowest elevation, is adjacent to the creek banks. Here, where the bubbly, slate-colored shores are often lined with oyster beds, the marshes' predominant "Spartina," or cordgrass, grows to its full height of 6 feet. The grasses in the low marsh, the transition zone from levee marsh to higher elevations, are shorter, 1 to 3 feet high.

The high marsh is where salt water covers the soil for only an hour or less each day. In this zone plant growth is severely limited. Even glasswort, saltwort, and salt grass, the hardiest salt-resistent plants, are absent in the high marsh's "salt pans," bare sandy areas where salt concentration reaches its peak.

In elevations slightly above the high marsh, freshwater run-off from nearby uplands creates a less saline environment. Needle rush and yellow-flowered sea oxyeye populate this brackish zone.

When the marsh abutts high elevations, there is little if any transition zone between water and climax forest. The graceful limbs of moss-laden live oaks shading the edge of the marsh creates the serene setting unique to southern marshlands.

Within the island's climax community, the live oak maritime forest, vegetation is diverse. Indigenous shrubs, vines, trees, and many introduced varieties share the island's rich alluvial soil. Over areas which were once cleared for farming, fallow fields have

naturally repropigated. Where hardwood forests have been disrupted by lumbering or fire, stands of pine have taken over. Many understory species, including ferns and saw palmetto, which is abundant from shore to shore, are dense along the forest floor.

Laurel oak, cabbage plam, tulip, sweet-gum, red maple, tupelo, southern magnolia, and dogwoods are among the trees that clamber over each other in the woodlands, but the majestic live oaks dominate them all. With limbs as long as 100 feet, these magical trees twist and curl, dip to the ground, and stretch into vaulted canopies. Some of the older oaks on the island have trunks as large as 35 feet in circumference. A variety of epiphytes (air plants) such as resurrection fern, several kinds of lichens (green and red), and bromeliads – Spanish moss and the rarer Tillandsia setecea – decorate the great oaks and other island trees.

Myriad wildflowers adorn the island with rainbows of red, yellow, blue, and purple. Native shrubs like "rattle box," oleanders, azalea honeysuckle, and hibiscus add their colorful blossoms as well. Red bud trees, fragrant gardenias, southern azaleas, and hundreds of other exotic plants have been introduced into the native bouquets. There is rarely a day that something is not in bloom on the island.

The islands' freshwater sloughs (temporary rain pools, ponds, and swamps) are critical to island wildlife. They are habitats for aquatic plants, water snakes, and amphibians; and oases for squirrels, rabbits, raccoons, opossums, deer, mink, otter, and even a few feral horses.

Because of the abundance of life surrounding the sloughs, predators such as alligators, rattlesnakes, and cottonmouth moccasins are attracted. On summer evenings, the raucous crescendos of frogs, toads, and peepers let everyone know they are there.

In the spring, island swamps become busy rookeries for egrets, herons, ibises, and woodstorks, only a few of the more than 300 species of birds that come to feed and nest in St. Simons' marshlands, along its shores, and in its forests.

HISTORY

THE EMERGENCE OF MAN

St. Simons' first human visitors were aboriginal Indians, anonymous nomads who roamed Georgia's pristine coast hunting, fishing, and feasting as they went. By the time history began to give an account of them, they had evolved into organized tribes and had begun to live in semi-permanent villages. Those who resided along Georgia's coast were known as Guale (pronounced *wallie*) Indians, a tribe of Lower Creeks.

The Guale's name originated with their Chief Guale who lived on St. Catherines Island. As was customary then, the chief's name also applied to the tribe's area of domain. Guale territory included Georgia's sea islands from St. Catherines to St. Andrews Sounds. The Guale called St. Simons Asao.

These were Indians of Muskhogean stock, tall, of good stature and tawny complexion. Their countenance was noble. Their features were strong and angular. The males wore their hair long and trussed it up turban fashion, often using it for storing arrows while hunting or engaging in war. They wore deerskin breechcloths and decorated their bodies with tatoos and temporary paints, especially for battle and ceremonial occasions.

One of their most noted ceremonies was the drinking of the "Black Drink," a council ritual. Only those who had proven themselves brave warriors were allowed to participate. The tea was made from the leaves of cassina, or *yaupon*, a native holly. It was empowering, but difficult to endure. Those who could stomach the noxious brew earned esteem and important commissions.

While the men hunted for game, smoked their pipes, and engaged in tribal politics, the women tended to cultivation and the rearing of children. They wore garments of feathers, skins, moss and leaves. Palm-leafed hats covered their heads. Their status was little better than that of a slave.

Monogomy was the standard, but there was one exception. The head chief could take two or more wives. His first was acknowledged as queen, and only her children became heirs.

Widows mourned the loss of their mate by cutting off their hair and scattering it over their departed's grave. They were not allowed to remarry until their hair grew long enough to cover their shoulders.

Because so many oyster shells were found in the Indians' kitchen middens, (their refuse heaps), we know that oysters were among their favorite foods. They also feasted on clams, fish, deer and other small game, fruits, berries, acorns, and corn from which they made a special bread.

Proof that an Indian village had been on Asao was confirmed in 1936. At that time archeologists, recommended by the Smithsonian Institute, came to St. Simons to examine skeletons and other artifacts that had been unearthed during the construction of the island's airport. The scientists' excavations revealed over 20,000 Indian artifacts, clay floors, and approximately 3,000 post molds, indications that there had been a large number of dwellings on the island.

They also confirmed that burials took place on St. Simons before the sixteenth century. After the early 1500s, Indian grave sites almost always contained brightly colored glass and beads, evidence of trade with the white man.

THE EUROPEANS

Spanish explorer Hernando De Soto was the first European to declare rights to Guale. He claimed the territory for Spain during his landmark expedition from Cuba through what is now Florida and the southeastern United States in 1538-1540.

The French ignored Spain's claim and became the first to attempt a colony in the area. Under the command of Hugenot Jean Ribault, their initial settlement was made in 1562 at Port Royal, S.C. It failed. Two years later, led by Loudonierre, they made a second at the mouth of the St. Johns River in Florida.

French encroachment on land Spain considered to be rightfully hers was not tolerated. By 1566 the Spanish had routed the French and nullified their place-names. *Ille de la Loire*, the name the French had given St. Simons, was again *Isla de Asao*. To alleviate further challenges to their claim, the Spanish began an active presence in the area.

As was customary for the Spaniards, who sought to conquer with "crossbow and cross," they sent soldiers and missionaries side by side into the new territory.[1] The first missionaries in Guale were Jesuit friars, but their effort was ill-fated. Plagued by murder, disease, and theological misunderstandings with the Indians, they were withdrawn by 1572. The Jesuits were replaced by Franciscans.

The Franciscan friars began to arrive in 1573. They too, encountered Indian resistance and hardship, but along with an increase in military might, their missionary zeal had effect. By 1595 they had established several sea island missions. Three sub-missions were on Asao: Octonico, Santo Domingo de Talaxe, and San Simon, the forebearer for the island's Anglicized name.

Spanish dominion prevailed in Guale until the latter half of the seventeenth century. When the Spaniards lost control, it was due to several pressures: pirates had become a menance, relations with the Indians were weak and stressed, and the English colonists to the north had become a problem. The English, who wanted the Indians' allegiance and lucrative trade, seized every opportunity to create trouble between the natives and the friars.

By 1680, the Spanish and English were openly hostile. Some Indians aligned with the Europeans and engaged in the conflict. Others were terrorized and fled. By 1686, only 417 Indians in nine villages remained of the 30,000 natives originally on the Georgia-Florida coast.[2]

In an attempt to prevent outright war, Spain and England signed a treaty which defined colonization rights by principle of occupation, but no exact boundaries were set. England clearly occupied territories north of, and including Charleston. Spain was entrenched in Florida, but had abandoned their missions in Guale as the Indian population declined.

Unoccupied, Guale became "the debatable land." Although the Spanish still considered Guale to be theirs, the English felt the claim was open to challenge. The area became the subject of much consideration abroad.

In 1717, Sir Robert Montgomery, a Scottish nobleman, published his *Discourse Concerning the Design'd Establishment of a New Colony*, an open invitation to wealthy Londoners to invest in the creation of a "Margravate of Azilia." The Azilia settlement was to include Ossabow, St. Catherines, Sapelo, and St. Simons Islands, a region to which he gave the "well deserved Denomination of the Golden Islands."[3] Sir Robert's dream did not materialize, but the English would not forget the Golden Isles.

Fifteen years later, in 1732, the English made a decisive move regarding the contested territory. Under the authority of King George II, a new colony was to be established between the Savannah and Altamaha Rivers. It was to be under the control of a twenty-one member board of trustees for twenty-one years, and was to be led by General James Edward Oglethorpe. In honor of King George II, the new colony was named Georgia.

The site for Georgia's first settlement was relatively near Charleston at Yamacraw Bluff, overlooking the Savannah River. To fortify against the Spanish, outposts were positioned down the coast as far south as Cumberland Island. The colony's second settlement, a military fort and town, was built near the Altamaha River's south branch on St. Simons Island. It was named Frederica in honor of Prince Frederick of Wales, son of King George II.

FREDERICA

Frederica was located on St. Simons' west bank at an advantageous bluff which overlooks river and marsh. Its strategic site had been recommended to General Oglethorpe by local Indians, with whom he shared mutual respect and legendary friendship.

Frederica's first group of colonists, thirty men, arrived on February 18, 1736. Their passage was aboard the sloop *Midnight*. The ship also carried a cargo of cannons, arms, ammunition, tools, and supplies. The remaining settlers arrived on March 7. By the end of the month, 44 men and 72 women and children had begun a new life on St. Simons Island.

While cannons guarded the river, Frederica's pioneers built a fort and a town. Permanent structures soon replaced their tents and huts. The majority of the construction was tabby, but some of the buildings contained brick which had been cargoed from England.

The fort was positioned along the river surveying northern and southern approaches. The towers on its bastions, each capable of holding one hundred men, were two stories high, and had mounted cannon.[4]

Behind the fort, toward the interior, was the town. It was patterned after a typical English village. Homes, which also contained shops, were built along two main intersecting streets and side streets. A palisaded wall and moat encircled the compound. Two gates guarded the entrances – one at the land-port, and one at the water-port.

Sentry and defense posts were established. Sentinel Richard Pike was stationed north of Frederica at a river point still known as "Pikes Bluff." An outpost named "New Hampton" was at the northwest tip of the island. Delegal's Fort, a temporary station on the south end of the island, later became the larger Fort St. Simons. A military road between the southern fort and Frederica was cut in three days.

Downriver from Frederica, Gascoigne Bluff provided anchorage for British ships. It is said to be Georgia's first naval base. This deep water area derived its name from Captian James Gascoigne of the *Hawk*, a sloop-

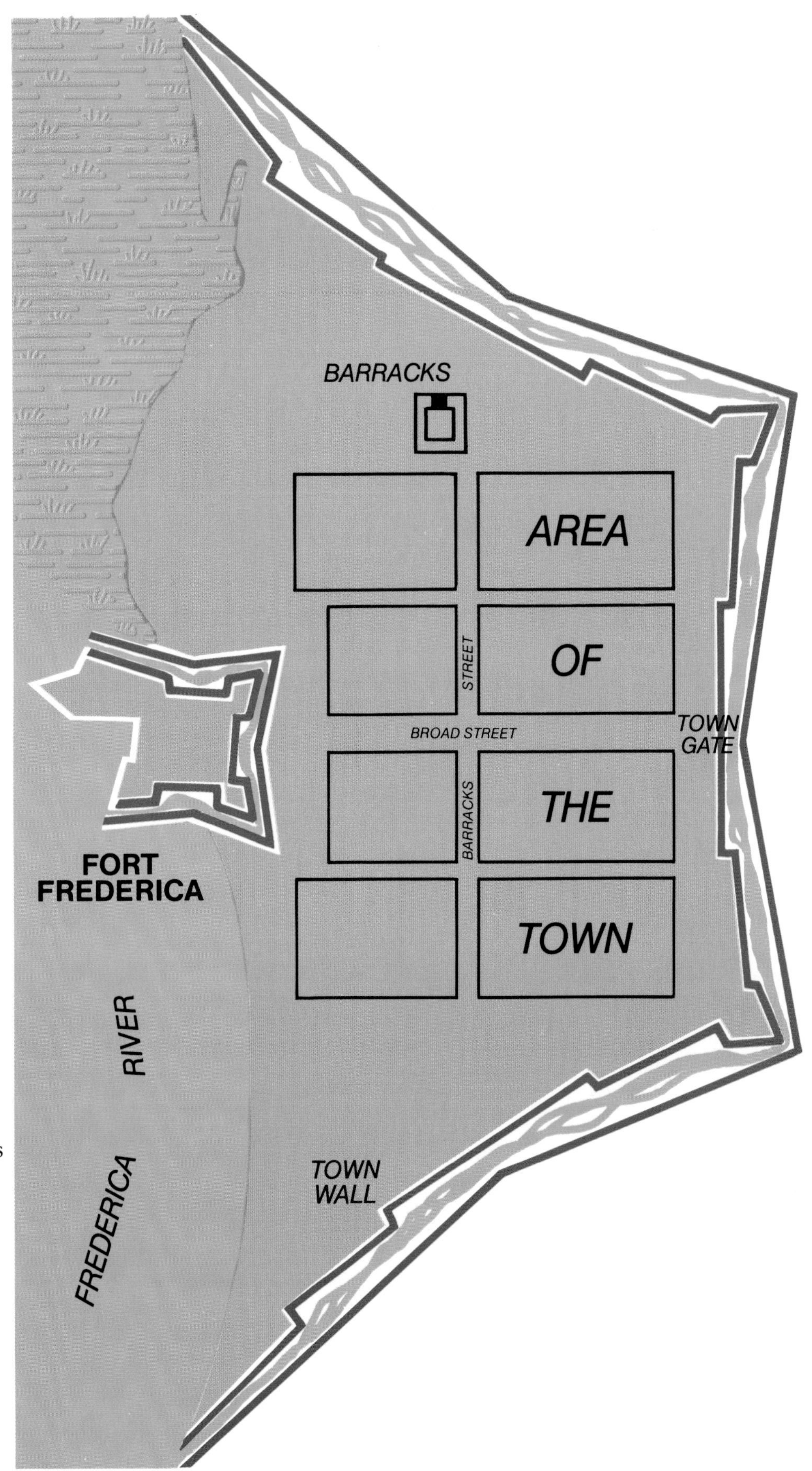

of-war that had convoyed many of the colonists from England.

Among Frederica's settlers were the names of Demere, Cannon, and Dunbar – names that appear on island streets today. Also among them were two young men who represented the official extension of The Church of England in the new colony, John and Charles Wesley.

THE WESLEYS

John Wesley, age 30, had ecclesiastical responsibilities for both Savannah and Frederica. He devoted most of his time to the larger, more established settlement. His brother Charles, age 25, performed pastoral duties in Frederica, and served as General Oglethorpe's secretary.

Charles Wesley's feelings about Frederica are reflected in the notes he made upon his arrival. He wrote, "I first set foot on St. Simons Island; and immediately my spirit revived. No sooner did I enter upon my ministry, than God gave me, like Saul, another heart."[5] While Charles was on St. Simons he held as many as four worship services a day.

After only three months at Frederica, Charles Wesley returned to England to deliver important dispatches from Oglethorpe to the colony's Trustees. Due to ill health, he never returned.

John Wesley made trips from Savannah to serve Frederica's congregation in Charles' absence. He visited St. Simons a total of five times, once while his younger brother was there.

The elder Wesley, erudite and devoted to a methodical faith, found little success at Frederica. His sermons, some of which contained admonitions against such things as hunting on Sunday, were not well received. After his last visit to the island, he lamented, "After having beaten the air in this unhappy place for twenty days, on January 26th (1737), I took my final leave of Frederica. It was not any apprehension of my own danger, but an utter dispair of doing good there, which made me content with the thought of seeing it no more."[6]

After one year and almost nine months in Georgia, John Wesley returned to England. There, in an ecclesiastical environment to which he was better suited, his convictions and efforts to reform the Anglican Church resulted in an evangelical movement that called itself Methodism.

THE SPANISH INVADE ST. SIMONS

Frederica's settlers were an industrious, independent group, more interested in survival than piety. In addition to the challenges of building a home from wilderness, they also had to contend with the ever present threat of Spanish invasion. When, in 1739, England declared war on Spain, the threat became imminent.

Frederica's peril intensified when the English, led by General Oglethorpe, attempted to invade St. Augustine in 1740. The effort was unsuccessful and politically humiliating to Oglethorpe. The General's reputation and ability to rally support for his colony suffered.

Georgia, Oglethorpe feared, was left to its own defenses. Even though he argued that if Georgia was to fall, the Carolinas and Virginia would be next, his petitions for help went unattended.

By this time, Frederica's population had reached 1,000, including the regiment of English Regulars stationed there. The fort had become Britian's largest, and perhaps most costly in North America.[7]

Oglethorpe's home "Orange Hall" was near Frederica. Captain Gascoigne had a 500 acre tract down the Frederica River on the island's southwest shore. Elsewhere on the island were the homes of a few others who were able to purchase private land grants. A group of Salzburgers had settled a few miles inland of Frederica in an area known as The Village.

Spain's expected counterattack came in the summer of 1742. Oglethorpe's defending troops, supplemented by Highland Rangers and Indians, numbered approximately 900. Estimates of the Spanish forces range from a "preposterous 5,000" to a more realistic number of 2,000.[8]

The Spanish fleet arrived on June 28, but waited seven days for favorable winds and tide before navigating the tricky channels into St. Simons Sound. When their vessels began to move, they soon outflanked the small number of defending ships, and avoided serious hits from Oglethorpe's batteries at Fort St. Simons. As Oglethorpe's troops retreated toward Frederica, the Spanish seized Fort St. Simons and made it their camp.

On July 7, the most important exchanges between the two armies developed. The day's events began when two Spanish columns were dispatched from Fort St. Simons in the direction of Frederica, each on a separate path. The two columns later converged, unintentionally, near an area known as Gully Hole Creek. Unknowingly, they had come within a mile and a half of Frederica.

The confused Spaniards were soon discovered. A small party of Rangers opened fire and sent word of the enemy's position to Oglethorpe at the fort. English reinforcements quickly joined the foray, and the Spaniards were "entirely routed."[9] When news of the incident reached the Spanish commander at Fort St. Simons, he sent three additional columns into the interior. In the skirmishes that followed, one became known as the "Battle of Bloody Marsh."

Spanish and English accounts of that day's events differ, but both agree that the legendary battle began as an ambush. British records say that their troops were deployed "facing a savannah or meadow through which the Spanish must pass on their way to Frederica."[10] The Spanish reported that they were fired upon while crossing "a causeway made of brush wood no wider than the trail."[11]

Oglethorpe admitted that the surprised Spaniards "fired with great spirit," but his men suffered no casualties.[12] The Spanish losses totaled seven men killed, eleven wounded. It was the last significant battle of the campaign.

After the Battle of Bloody Marsh, the Spanish retreated to Fort St. Simons. During the week that followed, English-allied Indians killed the crew of a Spanish ship that had been sent in search of fresh water. Three other Spanish vessels attempted to go up the Frederica River, but were deterred. Oglethorpe's troops crept within two miles of the Spanish camp, but were revealed when a soldier fired his weapon then deserted to the enemy camp.

Since Oglethorpe feared that the deserter would divulge the weakness of his army, he devised a counteraction. The General dispatched a letter to the informer indicating that he should continue to mislead the enemy. As anticipated, the letter was intercepted, but the Spanish were not

taken in by the elementary ploy. Nonetheless, it heightened their uncertainty. Both camps were fretful on July 13, when the unexpected gave Oglethorpe the decisive advantage. Five British ships were sighted north of St. Simons.

The next day the Spanish gave up their invasion. As one Spaniard noted, "It was not so much the five ships on the horizon that the Spanish feared as the unknown number that might lie just beyond."[13] Ironically, there were no other ships, and the five that were sighted were there only to gather information. The ships' captains had been ordered not to engage in hostilities.

Virtually unaided, Oglethorpe's troops had risen to the occasion. On July 14, the Spanish destroyed Fort St. Simons then sailed back to Florida. Soon after, Spain signed a treaty with England confirming the Crown's right to Guale. Because of Oglethorpe's victory on St. Simons Island, this part of America had an Anglo political and cultural destiny, rather than Spanish.

A TIME OF PEACE

Free from the threat of Spanish invasion, Frederica was no longer an important military fortification. This created panic among many of the merchants and craftsmen. They feared that their town would fall to ruins. In the peaceful years that followed, their predictions became reality.

When Oglethorpe returned to England in 1743, a reduced garrison was all that remained at Frederica. Eventually, all of Frederica's troops were withdrawn or disbanded. The townspeople also abandoned the settlement to build homes and farms on other areas of the island or on the mainland.

St. Simons changed, as did the entire colony, when its Trustee's charter expired in 1753. Georgia, which had been founded on the premise of providing a refuge for free, white, Protestant yeoman farmers, had been governed by rules unlike those of the other Royal colonies. In Georgia, black slave labor and whiskey trade with the Indians had been prohibited, and those who received land grants did not have the right to sell or give their land to anyone. Only the "tail male" provision (inheritance by the grantee's eldest son) applied.

Released from these special regulations, land owners began to sell their property. Several colonists on St. Simons began to acquire additional land and accumulated large estates. A few of them began using black slave labor.

Lumbering, farming, trade with the Indians, and a mercantile connection with England brought economic stability to St. Simons. The population was small, but the community flourished. All went well until the islanders faced another political crisis, the Revolutionary War.

AMERICA FIGHTS FOR INDEPENDENCE

When American Revolutionaries declared war on England, St. Simons' colonists were faced with a tough decision – whether to join the patriots or remain loyal to the Crown. The support they received from the mother country was difficult to deny. Many islanders became loyalists and moved to the West Indies, Florida, or other places to wait out the conflict. Those who became patriots left the island to join the Revolutionary forces, or moved inland. Only a few noncombatants remained on the island.

St. Simons was nearly deserted during most of the war; but, when in the spring of 1778, British troops attempted a landing near Pikes Bluff, a force of 300 patriots converged on the island, intercepted the British, and confiscated their ships. The patriots' victory on the island rallied Revolutionaries throughout the country.

In the fall of that same year, British ships again anchored offshore from Frederica. This time their commander reported that there were not a dozen men on St. Simons Island capable of bearing arms, and that those claimed to be British sympathizers. Uncontested, the British Regulars wreaked havoc on the defenseless community. Storehouses were torched. Farms were disrupted. Fort Frederica was dismantled and burned.

After America gained its independence,

a few islanders, both patriots and loyalists, returned to St. Simons. For all of them, it was a time to adjust to their losses and begin again. Among those who met the challenge were the pioneers of St. Simons' next prosperous period, the era of the great plantations, and sea island cotton.

COTTON ISLAND
ST. SIMONS' PLANTATION ERA

During the decade that followed the Revolution, St. Simons' planters developed a cotton crop that made agricultural history. Sea island cotton as it came to be known was the first strain of long staple cotton ever grown in America. Acclaimed as one of the finest cottons in the world, its excellent white color and long silky fibers earned top prices on the Liverpool market.

The famous cotton originated from a species grown on the island of Anguilla in the West Indies. After the Revolution, English provincials in the Bahamas cultivated "Anguilla" there, then shared their success by sending seeds back to their friends in Georgia. In 1886, St. Simons islander James Spalding received one of the first parcels of those seeds.

Spalding, a noncombatant loyalist who moved to Florida during the Revolution, had been a wealthy businessman before the war; but when he returned to St. Simons, he was near financial ruin. The warehouses and stores of his previous mercantile business had been destroyed. Through his business connections in the West Indies, he learned about the potential of "Anguilla," gathered the resources he had left, as well as the financial support of others, and invested in its cultivation. With the crop's success, he recouped his lost fortune and became one of the largest landowners in the county.

Major Alexander Bissett, St. Simons' first U.S. Senator, also pioneered the crop. He farmed the 500 acre tract originally granted to Captain James Gascoigne. When the Captain's fields were wrecked during the Spanish invasion, he returned to England. The property was then regranted to Major Bissett. Although the Major planted one of the first crops of sea island cotton ever grown, it was his successor, Richard Leake, who harvested it in 1788.

Another planter on St. Simons at that time was Raymond Demere, Jr. His plantation included land he inherited from his father, Captain Raymond Demere, commander at Frederica after General Oglethorpe returned to England. The family's homeplace, "Harrington Hall," was there. The junior Demere also owned "Mulberry Grove," property on the south end of the island where thousands of white mulberry trees had been planted to feed silk worms,

the tiny laborers of the industry anticipated by the early colonists.

As St. Simons' first planters moved away or died, island land passed into the possession of newcomers. Among them were Oxford graduates, statesmen, international businessmen, and military men – a well traveled, distinguished group.

Although the island planters earned sizable profits, most of them elected to live in understated luxury. Compared to many of the era's opulent plantation homes, those on St. Simons were relatively modest. In regard to island hospitality, however, little was held in reserve. As a newspaper article of the day attested, "If the health of the St. Simons planters should keep pace with their hospitality, they will each see their hundreth year."[14]

Common enterprise and semi-seclusion encouraged a close community among the planters. Their society was that of a gentlemen's culture. They gathered in each others homes to share sumptuous meals, introduce guests, discuss their work, politics, philosophy, and community interests.

Several planters joined the effort to organize the island's first church, Christ Church, Frederica, the second oldest Episcopal church in the Diocese of Georgia. It was incorporated by an act of State Legislature in 1808.

Many family gatherings revolved around the church. In addition to worship and ministry, church functions provided regular opportunities for the exchange of ideas, news and gossip. The church's first building, erected by the planters in 1820, served its congregation until it was ruined during the Civil War.

On special occasions, such as the Fourth of July, plantation families gathered to celebrate in Frederica, or "Old Town," as it had come to be known. After Brunswick became the county seat in 1797, Frederica, though practically deserted, remained the island's post town and gathering place for a few more years.

The island plantations were built and worked in the established southern tradition, requiring many slaves to tend their huge fields.[15] Many of the slaves were relocated to St. Simons from other plantations; others were bought directly from their captors.

Although the plantation slaves had a common West African heritage, they represented many different tribes of origin and customs. Among them were Mohamedans who read and wrote in Arabic, and others whose tribal speech influenced the southern dialect. Their native languages, such as Kimbundu, Tshiluba, Vai, Wolof, Twi, Kingo, and Ibo, crossbred with English to bring expressions like goober, gumbo, chigger, tote, nana, and biddy, into common usage.

In 1798, the importation of African slaves was prohibited in Georgia, but the legislation did not stop the practice. Slave traders continued to bring in their human merchandise, often landing their illicit cargoes along the winding creeks and waterways of coastal Georgia. Ebo Landing on St. Simons' Dunbar Creek was reputed to be one of their best havens. Folk lore recounts that the landing's name originated with a group of captives from the Ebo, or Ibo, tribe. While being unloaded there, the legend says, these proud men chose to walk into the water and drown themselves rather than be sold into slavery.

A separate plantation culture, with a well defined caste system, developed among those who did become slaves. The butler, cook, maids, children's nurses, and other house servants were at the top of the order. Next came the artisans – carpenters, blacksmiths, seamstresses, and nurses for the sick. Those with the least community power were the field hands.

When the British occupied the island for three weeks during the War of 1812, some slaves took refuge on the mainland with their owners; others went with, or were taken by the British, who also took cattle, cotton, food, equipment, and other valuables. It was a setback but plantation life resumed.

As many as fifteen plantations contributed to St. Simons' saga as "cotton island." Among the more successful were Retreat, Hamilton, Cannon's Point, Hampton, Kelvin Grove, St. Clair and Black Banks, West Point, and Orange Grove.

RETREAT PLANTATION
Retreat, perhaps the island's most famous plantation, was located on the south end of the island. It was on land that once belonged to James Spalding. After Spalding's death, Major William Page from Page's Point, South Carolina, bought the plantation. He and his wife gave Retreat its name. Their only child, Anne Page King, inherited the property and managed it admirably. Her husband, Thomas Butler King, was a member of the House of Representatives and chairman of the House Naval Committee. His duties often called him away from the plantation. Many notables, including John James Audubon, were guests at Retreat.

During the Civil War epoch, when St. Simons had no lighthouse, mariners navigated by Retreat's four-story cotton barn. U.S. Geodetic maps of the day identified it as "King's Cotton House."

Retreat remained in the King family until the 1920s. It then became the grounds for the Sea Island Golf Club. Tabby ruins from the Retreat era are among the golf course's greens and fairways. The plantation's corn barn has been incorporated into the clubhouse.

HAMILTON PLANTATION
In 1793, the property at Gascoigne Bluff became Hamilton Plantation when James Hamilton, a South Carolina planter, London merchant, and one of the country's first millionaires, bought the plantation from Richard Leake.

Because of the plantation's location along the deep water channels of the Frederica River its wharves were important lading points. In 1794, prized island live oak, including timber cut on Hamilton, was shipped from Gascoigne Bluff to Boston where shipbuilders used the wood to build *The U.S.S. Constitution*, one of the U.S. Navy's first battleships. St. Simons' tough live oaks earned this vessel the name of *Old Ironsides*. It is still afloat today.

Although James Hamilton was often away from the island due to his widespread business interests, he nevertheless made important contributions to the small community. He was active in civic affairs, became one of Christ Church's first vestrymen, and earned the reputation of being one of the finest gentlemen on the island.

When James Hamilton moved his residence from St. Simons to Philadelphia, his plantation passed into the possession of his namesake and business partner's son, James Hamilton Couper. The Couper family retain-

ed the property until after the Civil War.

Hamilton's next owners were Norman W. Dodge, son of philanthropist William E. Dodge of New York City, and Titus G. Meigs also of New York. Under their ownership the plantation property became the site of the country's third largest sawmill operation. A thriving mill town developed around this enterprise and remained active through the turn of the 20th century.

After the sawmills closed, a financier from Detroit, Eugene W. Lewis, bought Hamilton and restored much of the old plantation to its former grandeur.

In 1949, the Methodist Church's South Georgia Conference Center Commission bought a large portion of Hamilton and established Epworth By The Sea, The Methodist Center. Thousands of people have since come to Epworth for conferences, retreats, and vacations.

Three of the plantation's tabby slave cabins still stand. One is in use by the Methodist Center. The other two are maintained by the Cassina Garden Club.

CANNON'S POINT PLANTATION

Cannon's Point, property that lay between the Hampton River and Jones Creek, derived its name from its original grantee, Daniel Cannon, carpenter at Frederica. After the Revolutionary War, it became the property of John Couper, James Hamilton's business partner.

John Couper, signer of Georgia's constitution, was a remarkable man. Cultured, witty, and of the highest integrity, his legendary hospitality entertained many of the most prominent men in the United States and Europe. He was civic minded, a vestryman of Christ Church, and one of the world's leading agriculturists.

Under Couper's ownership, Cannon's Point became a showcase for exquisite gardens and experimental crops. He planted every variety of grape known at that time, date palms, lemons, oranges, sugar cane, and olive trees. His cotton fields were developed to perfection. A Cannon's Point live oak provided the original sternposts for *Old Ironsides*.

Natural disasters compelled Couper to sell many of his scattered landholdings, but he did not relinquish the property at Cannon's Point. It remained in his family until after the Civil War.

The three story plantation home at Cannon's Point burned near the turn of the twentieth century. Its tabby ruins and surrounding acreage have been left undisturbed by Cannon's Point's current owner, The Sea Island Company.

HAMPTON PLANTATION

In 1758 the property that came to be known as Hampton Plantation was granted to Henry Ellis, Georgia's second Royal Governor. The next owner was Lieutenant Philip Delegal. In 1774, the property was sold to Major Pierce Butler, a politically influential South Carolinian.

Unlike his easy-going unpretentious neighbors, Major Butler was an austere man who conducted his affairs with formality. Under his regimented style, Hampton developed into one of the most notable and luxurious plantations on the island.

Hampton's reputation was perhaps as much effected by two notorious guests as by its prosperity. The two visitors were Vice President Aaron Burr and Frances Anne (Fanny) Kemble, English actress and writer of a diary that some credit as having swayed the outcome of the Civil War.

Vice President Burr visited Hampton after killing Alexander Hamilton in their famous duel. Highly censured for his action in the North, he came south to Hampton where the duel was still considered a gentleman's option.

Fanny Kemball, the toast of London and Parisian society, came to Hampton in the spring of 1839, after she and her husband, the Major's grandson, Pierce Butler, II, had wintered on the Butler Island rice plantation. During her stay she recorded her experiences in a dairy entitled *Journal of a Residence on a Georgia Plantation in 1838-1839*. Her words praised the area's beauty but condemned the system which used slave labor. When her *Journal* was published in 1863, its impassioned condemnation of the southern plantation way of life is said to have taken European and American sympathies away from the Confederate cause permanently.[16]

KELVIN GROVE PLANTATION

Kelvin Grove Plantation, home of the Cater-Armstrong-Postell family, contained more than 1600 acres of the island's cleared and cultivated land, timberland, meadow marsh, and beach property.[17] Its boundaries included the site of the Battle of Bloody Marsh and several miles of the oldest continuously used road on St. Simons, the Military Road which was cut during colonial days.

The U.S. Coast Guard Station, Massengale Park, and The King and Prince Hotel are on property that was once Kelvin Grove, as is the Malcolm McKinnon Airport, and several residential communities, including its namesake Kelvin Grove, The Meadows, Wesley Oaks, Broadway, Peachtree, Oglethorpe Park, East Beach, and Highland Acres.

ST. CLAIR PLANTATION AND BLACK BANKS

Soon after the War of 1812, Massachusetts native, James Gould, builder of St. Simons' first lighthouse, bought 900 acres of land that lay across the center of the island from the Black Banks River to Dunbar Creek. This property was named St. Clair. Gould later bought another 600 adjoining acres that became Black Banks Plantation.

Prior to building a home on St. Clair, the Gould family lived in the keeper's cottage at the foot of the lighthouse. In addition to building the lighthouse, Gould served as its keeper for twenty-seven years.

When Christ Church was first built, Gould was one of its wardens. Both of his sons, James F., and Horace B. Gould, later served as vestrymen. After Christ Church was destroyed during the Civil War, the congregation held services at Black Banks, which had become the home of Horace Gould.

Today, some of the grounds of St. Clair and Black Banks are still in the possession of

Gould's descendents. The Black Banks home is the oldest occupied residential structure on the island. On other lands of the former plantation are the St. Clair residential community and the Sea Palms Golf and Tennis Resort.

WEST POINT PLANTATION

West Point Plantation, a tract of property north of Frederica, once belonged to James Spalding and his senior partner, Donald Mackay. In 1818 it was bought by Colonial William Hazzard. The Colonel's younger brother, Dr. Thomas Hazzard, owned Pike's Bluff, an adjoining plantation which included Richard Pike's colonial sentry post.

In 1838, Dr. Hazzard shot John Wylly of the neighboring Village Plantation over a boundary dispute. He was tried for manslaughter, but was not convicted. Nonetheless, because of community criticism and personal guilt, he would no longer attend Christ Church, where he was a vestryman and his brother a warden. Instead, he built a private place of worship that came to be known as "Pink Chapel." The structure's stone facade took on a pink hue because of a lichen, but plantation slaves said the chapel turned pink because their master had blood on his hands.

When Dr. Hazzard died in 1849, his older brother operated Pike's Bluff along with West Point. Today, these properties are the grounds of privately owned estates.

ORANGE GROVE PLANTATION

South of Frederica along Dunbar Creek, John Terry, silversmith and recorder at Frederica, planted hundreds of orange trees and appropriately named his tract "Orange Grove." When he vacated the property, it was regranted to James Bruce, a Savannah merchant who also owned a lot in Frederica. The property passed into the possession of Bruce's daughter Rebecca, who married Major Samuel Wright of Savannah. Although the property was sold shortly after the Civil War, a direct descendent of the Wright family regained possession of Orange Grove in 1929. Today, it is a part of the Sea Palms West development.

THE PLANTATION ERA COMES TO AN END

St. Simons' planters met with a variety of crises through the years. Hurricanes, plagues of caterpillers, boll weevils, wars, and volatile markets tested their resources. By the time third generation growers were in command, the challenges had become intense. Fields were impoverished and less productive. Cotton prices were low. The use of slave labor had become increasingly controversial. With the onset of the Civil War, the difficulties became insurmountable. The plantation economy soon collapsed.

When Georgia seceded from the Union in January 1861, most of the men on the island left to serve the Confederacy. Women, children, a few older men, and slaves carried on a similitude of plantation life until Federal gunboats blockaded the Georgia coast in December of that same year. At that time, Confederate forces were positioned on the south end of St. Simons to defend Brunswick harbor. Civilians, ordered to evacuate, quickly buried their silver and other valuables, then left for the mainland on crowded boats and rafts.

Within two months the Confederate forces relinquished St. Simons. In their retreat they exploded the island's lighthouse to deny its aid to Federal ships. For the remainder of the war Union troops occupied the island.

During Federal occupation, most everything of value on the island was plundered, abused, or destroyed. Homes were ransacked. Fencing was burned for firewood. Stray stock trampled gardens and lawns. Christ Church, used as a campsite and slaughterhouse, was ruined. The island also became a concentration area for freed slaves, or "contraband," as they were called.

RECONSTRUCTION

America's most tragic war was a cruel and heartbreaking time for Confederates and Unionists alike. But, when the fighting stopped, the nightmare did not end in the defeated South.

The war's devestation hung like a dark cloud over St. Simons. For awhile, circumstances were dire. Everyone on the island had to depend on food supplied by the Federal government.

Many former plantation families were in chaos. The Federal government had granted vacated lands to homeless slaves, and the process of reclaiming ownership was mired in confusion. Northern "carpetbaggers" exploited the situation and added to the frustration. Many families gave up, moved away, and left the remnants of their old life behind. Some managed to recoup their property and tried to farm, but their untended fields, overgrown and parched, would never again cultivate the crop for which they became famous.

In the 1880s rays of hope began to penetrate the darkness. A new lighthouse literally began to shine in 1882, and a new economy was on the horizon.

The island began to revitalize when New Yorkers, Norman W. Dodge and Titus G. Meigs bought Hamilton Plantation for the Dodge-Meigs Lumber Mills. Timber cut from the company's vast landholdings in middle Georgia was floated down the Altamaha River to Darien, then brought to St. Simons for sawing and shipping.

Jobs were no longer scarce. There were four mills to be operated: the Big Mill, the Planing Mill, the Cypress Mill, and the Lower mill. The huge operation became the third largest sawmill center in America. As many as 20 ships at one time would be anchored off Gascoigne Bluff awaiting their cargoes of lumber.

The former plantation became a bustling mill town. The old plantation house became a boarding house; the cotton barn, a general merchandise store and post office; slave cabins, support buildings. New buildings went up, too: houses for officials and workers, the island's first school, and the St. James Union Church, which is today Epworth By the Sea's Lovely Lane Chapel.

The Dodge-Meigs contribution to the island was not limited to its economic impact. It brought the benefit of human resources as well. Norman Dodge's son, Anson Green Phelps Dodge, fell in love with St. Simons during a visit and made the

island his home. He was exceptionally generous with his wealth and personal service. He endowed the rebuilding of Christ Church, which was dedicated as a memorial to his first wife, then became the rebuilt church's first rector. After he and his second wife, Anna Gould, granddaughter of lighthouse builder James Gould, experienced the loss of their infant son, the Reverend built an orphanage, The Dodge Home for Boys, as a memorial to him.

EARLY RESORT DAYS

While the island enjoyed the economic stability created by the sawmills, the foundation for a tourist industry was being laid. As the mills' business brought sojourners, accommodations were built, transportation was improved, and word of St. Simons' intrigue spread.

In 1887, a pier was constructed off the south end of the island near the new lighthouse. Rails were laid on the pier and up the length of "Railway Avenue," an oceanside strip which led to boarding houses, summer cottages, and grand hotels. Until they were replaced by a steam engine, two donkeys pulled an open air trolley that carried guests along the tracks.

Passenger boats *Sea Gate, Emmeline, Hessie, Attaquin*, and a side-wheeler, *The City of Brunswick*, provided regular ferry service from Brunswick.

The island began to receive more national guests after Sidney Lanier's famous poem "The Marshes of Glynn," was published in 1878, but most of the island's visitors were regional. A cluster of beachside cottages known as the "Waycross Colony," attested to the number of families who came from this nearby South-Georgia town.

As tourism increased, the center of island activity began to shift from the banks of the Frederica River to the oceanside village. Concurrently, the sawmills' natural resource was becoming depleted. The sawing slowed, then came to a complete stop in the 1920s. There were, however, ambitious new plans for Gascoigne Bluff. It was to be the access point for a highway from the mainland.

The Brunswick-St. Simons Highway became a reality and was formally opened on July 11, 1924. According to an announcement folder distributed by the Southern Railway System, "the wonderful engineering feat, which cost nearly half a million dollars, eliminates the boat ride from Brunswick, and makes St. Simons one of the most accessible resorts on the South Atlantic Coast."[18] There was much fanfare and celebration – a historical peagent, a parade, fish dinners, and addresses by state and local dignitaries.

Detroit financial giants, Howard Coffin and Eugene W. Lewis, were among the visionaries who anticipated St. Simons' potential once it became accessible by automobile. These two friends acquired several properties in the area and became instrumental to St. Simons' future.

Eugene Lewis, founder of the Industrial National Bank of Detroit, became interested in coastal Georgia as a result of his friendship with Howard Coffin. When Coffin introduced him to the beauty of St. Simons, the land that became most dear to him was the old Hamilton Plantation property. After the lumber mills closed, Lewis purchased the property and reinstated it to much of its former grandeur.

Howard Coffin, a pioneer in automobiles and aircraft, had different plans for some of St. Simons' old cotton fields. On grounds that were once Retreat Plantation, he created the Sea Island Golf Club. To give golfers and guests better access to the club, he cut Kings Way, a road from the new causeway to the south end of the island. He also developed the legendary 5-Star, 5-Diamond, Cloister Hotel and Resort across the Black River on neighboring Long Island, which he renamed Sea Island. Today, a large portion of St. Simons is still owned and managed by the extant company of Howard Coffin, The Sea Island Company.

The future tourist industry Coffin anticipated for St. Simons was interrupted by the great depression of the 1930s. Few Americans could afford the luxury of travel. Even so, St. Simons was not at a standstill. The island's small population continued a slow, but steady growth. Creative geniuses such as artist Maxfield Parrish began to live and work amid the inspiration of the island's tranquility, as did other professionals and the quiet rich.

As the community grew, it diversified. Christ Church no longer served everyone. Persons of the Baptist, Methodist, and Presbyterian persuasions worshipped in a new interdenominational church. Soon, each of these groups had their own buildings. St. Williams, a Roman Catholic Chapel held services on Frederica Road.

The post office was in the village where a few small stores provided essential supplies and services. Everett Grocery, the general store, also served as a bank. Nearby, a private beachside club, The King and The

Prince, was developed by J. Franklin Horn and Morgan Wynn in 1935. Six year later, the facility opened its doors to the public as The King and Prince Beach Hotel-Club. It was a short season, however. German U-boats were sighted off Georgia's coast. World War II had gripped the nation.

Men in uniform became a familiar sight on the island. The U.S. Navy occupied The King and Prince, and only a few miles away, there were thousands of military men stationed at Camp Stewart, and thousands more in Savannah and Jacksonville. Hundreds of these soldiers discovered St. Simons while on leave. After the war, many returned as vacationers, others made the island their post war home.

The influx of veterans and their families spurred growth. Enterprise responded. New homes, hotels, motels, and resort facilities began to be woven into the old. Near Gascoigne Bluff, Epworth By The Sea, The Methodist Center, began to provide accommodations for retreats, youth camps, and a retirement community for its ministers.

As the island's popularity continued to grow, its entertainment and recreational community kept a contemporary pace. Sea Palms Golf and Tennis Resort, an 800-acre center for conferences and retreats with 27 holes of golf, and a 12 court racquet club was added, as was the St. Simons Island Club, which offers 18 holes of golf and tennis.

Other facilities were expanded. The King and Prince became a 4-Star hotel with villas, meeting and convention facilities, ballroom, and recreational accouterments. The Sea Island Golf Club which now offers 36 holes of golf, earned national recognition with its Seaside Course. Seaside's number four hole is acclaimed among the top 100 rated holes of golf in U.S. In the words of famous golfer Bobby Jones, "The (Sea Island Golf Club's) Seaside Course is one of the greatest nine holes of golf I've ever played."

In addition to tennis and championship golf, the island has marinas bristling with yachts, parks, swimming pools, heath clubs and spas, an equestrian stable, bicycle and boat rentals, fish camps, and guided nature tours. There are less active pleasures as well: art galleries, community theater, concerts, lectures, and many special interest events.

The island's cultural community also became rich with famous artists and best selling authors. Several great and upcoming talents are members of the island's art colony.

While the village, at the intersection of Mallory Street and Ocean Boulevard, remained the seaside hub of commerce and public recreation, a variety of restaurants, shopping malls, boutiques, and specialty shops nestled among the oaks in other areas as well, especially along Frederica Road.

Although St. Simons became more modern, times long past and people long gone are still engendered in the island spirit. Several streets and enterprises carry nostalgic names – Black Banks, Couper, Demere, Dunbar, Hampton, St. Clair, and The Emmeline and Hessie are among the more familiar.

Island celebrations keep tradition alive as well. The Fourth of July is always a big event. In August, The Sea Island Festival pays special tribute to the people who provided the muscle for the island's plantation days.

A year-round step into the past can be enjoyed at the Museum of Coastal History, headquartered at the foot of the lighthouse in the old keepers cottage. The Museum houses a collection of colonial furniture, household articles, shipbuilding tools, and other fascinating artifacts from the island's history. Both the restored keeper's cottage and the lighthouse are on the National Register of Historic Places. They are said to be the oldest brick structures in Glynn County.

Fort Frederica National Monument also offers the history-lover a thrill of authenticity. The National Park Service has engineered excavations, field exhibits, video presentation, and artifact displays to give a first hand impression of what life was like in colonial days.

Life on the island today integrates old and new with a singular and pleasing effect: it feels like home. Regardless of background or lifestyle, talent or wealth, it is a welcoming, comfortable haven. The island has changed through the years, but it has not surrendered its magic, nor its gift to bestow contentment.

Present-day islanders readily share their treasured paradise, but some, fearful of unbridled growth, are apprehensive about the island's future. As the island continues to invite and enthrall, those who love St. Simons will be called upon to address issues which will effect its landscape. As more strangers become visitors, and more visitors become residents, entrepreneural enthusiasm will require negotiation. Change will be an ongoing process.

With vision and a passionate committment to the wellbeing of this extraordinary place, perhaps St. Simons' human friends will preserve its essence for generations yet to come. St. Simons Island has never been a static environment. It has been changing since the moment of its creation, and it is still a world apart where the mystery of an enchanted island night and the beauty of an island dawn are but preludes to the endless subtle and sublime qualities that keep drawing us back.

"I observed here a kind of long moss I had never seen before; it grows in great quantities upon the large trees, and hangs down three or four yards from the boughs; it gives a noble, ancient, and hoary look to the woods; it is of a whitish green color, but when dried is black and like horsehair. This the Indians use for wadding their guns, and making their couches soft under the skins of beasts which serve them for beds. They use it also for tinder, striking fire by flashing the pans of their guns into a handful of it, and for all other uses where old linen would be necessary."

Francis Moore on Spanish moss
A Voyage to Georgia

Snowy egret

Shanty

Neptune Park

Sailboats, Massengale Beach

HOBIE 16

Island Sunset

The King and Prince Beach Hotel and Villas

Woodstorks

Marsh and Little St. Simons Island

Bridge fishing

And the marsh is meshed with a million veins,
That like as with rosy and silvery essences flow
In the rose-and-silver evening glow.
Farewell, my lord sun!
The creeks overflow: a thousand rivulets run
"Twixt the roots of the sod; the blades of the marsh-grass
stir;
Passeth a hurrying sound of wings that westward whirr;
Passeth, and all is still; and the currents cease to run;
And the sea and the marsh are one.

How still the plains of the waters be
The tide is in his ecstasy.
The tide is at his highest height:
And it is night.

And now from the Vast of the Lord will the waters of sleep
Roll in on the souls of men,
But who will reveal to our waking ken
The forms that swim and the shapes that creep
Under the waters of sleep?
And I would I could know what swimmeth below when the
tide comes in
On the length and the breadth of the marvellous marshes
of Glynn.

Excerpt: "The Marshes of Glynn," Sidney Lanier, 1878

Mainland view, Marshes of Glynn

Dunes, East Beach

Frederica River shrimp boat dock, former site of the Sea Island Yacht Club

Village

Beach house

Seagulls

The St. Simons Lighthouse is a cherished landmark symbol for the Golden Isles. Tall, perfectly proportioned, and dazzling white, it is one of the most beautiful beacons on the Atlantic Coast. It is 106 feet high, equipped with its original *Fresnel* lens, and sends a 500,000 candle power beam visible 18 miles at sea. It has served navigators since 1872, but it is not St. Simons' first lighthouse.

There have been two lighthouses in St. Simons' history. The first one, a 75 foot tall, octagonal structure, was built in 1811 by James Gould, who also became its keeper. Gould's lighthouse was operational until the Civil War when retreating Confederate soldiers destroyed it to deny its aid to enemy ships.

The lighthouse standing today was designed and built during the Reconstruction Era by Charles B. Cluskey. Cluskey, a noted architect from Savannah, also built the nine room keeper's cottage at the tower's base.

Both lighthouses were erected near the same site on Couper's Point, land which provides an excellent vantage of St. Simons Sound and the open sea. Colonial Fort St. Simons and the Confederate army's Fort Brown were located here. In the 1790s, when the government first sought land for the purpose of building a lighthouse, John Couper of Cannon's Point owned the property. He deeded the government the needed land, a four-acre parcel, for the sum of one dollar.

Before electricity, when the beacon was powered by kerosene, a keeper's constant attention was needed to remove soot build-up from the lantern and to relight it when gusty winds extinguished the flame. According to island legend, the invisible presence of one early keeper, one who was murdered by his assistant, returns to see that the light is being cared for properly. The tale points out that the ghostly footsteps are especially loud during storms, as though the dutiful keeper is there to lend a hand in case of trouble.

The last St. Simons' lighthouse keeper retired in 1950. The automatic light is now operated and maintained by the United States Coast Guard. Both the lighthouse and the restored keeper's cottage, which now houses the Museum of Coastal History, are on the National Register of Historic Places. They are said to be the oldest brick structures in Glynn County.

St. Simons Island Lighthouse, Sunrise

Twilight

Shrimp boat

Sunrise

Village pier

Pier

Barn

"In the early days, the old drawbridges of the Brunswick-St. Simons causeway required manpower to operate them. When the wind was strong and gusty, it was too difficult for a bridge keeper to swing out the bridge by himself. A driver from one of the cars would have to get out and help him turn the winch."

"Not many of us lived on the island back in the 1930s and 40s, so strangers were always of interest and something of an event. The mechanic in the village had an axle hanging in front of his garage. When an unknown attractive female was in the area, he would come out and clang that axle with his wrench giving us locals the signal. The visitor wouldn't know it, but nearly everyone would come out to take a look at her."

"In the late 1920s, when I was about nine years old, I loved to go crabbing. My favorite place was off the pier. It was wooden then, and had two levels. The upper level had an enclosed area with a dance floor. Social events there were very popular. Boats were docked at the lower level. I was almost always there. If I didn't want the crabs I caught, I sold them for a nickle each. There was always a buyer."

"Before we had the Malcolm McKinnon Airport, Redfern Field was the island's landing strip. It bordered Frederica Road, which was then made of crushed shell and sand. Airplanes like the *Tin Goose* and *Gypsy Moth* would land, taxi across Frederica Road, then lumber to a stop under the big oaks near Shug's, a popular island pub."

— *Reminiscent Islanders*

Sea Island Stables

Sea Island Stables

Island pasture

Wildflowers, Sea Island Causeway

Christ Church, Frederica is the second oldest Episcopal church in the Diocese of Georgia. It was organized by a group of St. Simons planters in 1807. The following year it was incorporated by Act of State Legislature. One hundred acres of the commons of Frederica and three lots from within the town were granted for the church's use.

The church's first building, erected in 1820, was a small, white structure with green shutters and a belfry. During the Civil War, Federal troops occupied the chapel and left it in ruins – pews burned, organ smashed, windows shattered, its altar used as a butcher block.

The desecrated church remained in shambles until 1886, when Reverend Anson G. P. Dodge, Jr., son of Norman Dodge of the Dodge-Meigs Lumber Company, endowed the rebuilding of the church as a memorial to his first wife.

Located on the same site and cornerstone as the first, the present church is cruciform in design, with trussed Gothic roof, and steepled belfry. Stained glass windows, given as memorials, commemorate incidents in the life of Christ and the early history of the church on St. Simons. Part of the original Credence Table and an inset from the first church's altar are preserved in the existing altar.

In the old churchyard, under the serenity of magnificent live oak canopies, are the headstones of many who have been a part of St. Simons' history. The oldest stone is dated 1803, but it is thought that much earlier burials took place here.

Christ Church, Frederica

Christ Church Cemetery

Christ Church Cemetery

Seabreezes swell and subside along St. Simons shores and in its forests. Many years ago, a beautiful young woman named Mary felt their freshness. Evening and night, with lantern in hand, she combed the island's moss spun grounds for signs of her betrothed. But, her search was in vain. His boat capsized off St. Simons' beach, her husband-to-be was lost forever to the sea. Stricken with grief, Mary took her life. But even after her suicide, Mary's luminous form could still be seen making the futile rounds. As the plantation slaves noted, "Mary, she wanda," and continues to do so even until this day, or so the legend goes.

Commorant

Marsh

Abandoned dock, former site of the Frederica Yacht Club

St. Simons' Ebo Landing on Dunbar Creek, which is now a vacant lot, received its name when a group of African captives from the Ebo, or Ibo, tribe were brought here and chose to drown themselves rather than be sold into slavery. As they were unloaded from the ship, these proud men marched together into the deep waters of the creek, chanting: "the water brought us in, the water will take us away," or so the legend goes.

White fallow deer

Marsh snail

There is nothing quite like being in the presence of live oak trees. Their huge, languid limbs, some as long as 100 feet, dip, contort, and stretch into lofty canopies. With misty festoons of Spanish moss draping from nearly every bough, their magic spreads enchantment across the island.

Live oak tree

St. Simons Island Club

Great blue heron

The Tabby House, former slave cabin

Flower garden, Sea Palms Golf and Tennis Resort

Coastal Indians feasted on oysters and discarded their shells in refuse mounds known as oyster middens, shell middens, and kitchen middens. Due to the Indians' great appetite for oysters, their middens became a valuable resource for the making of tabby, a construction material used extensively by early European settlers.

The word *tabby* (tappi or tabbi) is thought to be African in origin, with Arabic background. It means a wall made of earth or masonry. To build with tabby, the settlers would mix a mortar of lime, oyster shells, sand, and water, then pour it into wooden forms.

The Spanish who pioneered St. Augustine are credited with bringing the tabby process to North America. English settlers then acquired the skill and built tabby structures all along the southeastern coast, first in Charleston, later Savannah, then in Frederica.

To produce lime, tabby's bonding agent, oyster shells were burned in lime kilns. In Frederica, lime burnings were grand social occasions. As many as 200 to 300 bushels of oyster shells would be burned at one time. The festivities would usually begin around four or five in the afternoon, last well past midnight, and allow the colonists their favorite indulgences; namely, biscuits and honey, tea, beer, and wine.

Tabby barn, Taylor's Fish Camp

St. Ignatius Episcopal Church

Slave cabins, Gascoigne Bluff

Sunset,
Epworth By The Sea,
Gascoigne Bluff

It is fitting that Epworth By The Sea, The Methodist Center, is located on St. Simons Island. Here, the denomination's founding fathers, the Wesley brothers, John and Charles, served as Anglican missionaries and ministers to Frederica's first colonists. Named to commemorate the Wesley's birth place, Epworth, England, Epworth By The Sea welcomed its first campers and guests in 1950. It is located on grounds that were once Hamilton Plantation.

Lovely Lane Chapel, Epworth By The Sea

St. Simons Island Marina

U.S. Coast Guard Station, Frederica River

Marsh

Great egret

Taylor's Fish Camp

Island commerce

Edward Teach the pirate, better known as Blackbeard, is said to have roamed the sea island waterways, burying his booty perhaps on St. Simons Island. Lured by the possibility, treasure hunters are still attempting to find it.

Frederica River

Alligator

Frederica River

The synergy of St. Simons' natural beauty is as mesmerizing as dawn and as welcoming as an outstretched hand. Endlessly intriguing, it invites for a day or a lifetime.

Sea Island Golf Club

Fairway, Sea Island Golf Course

Retreat Plantation slave hospital, Sea Island Golf Club

Sea Island Golf Club's Avenue of Oaks, planted during Retreat Plantation era

Garden

St. Simons Island enjoys a semi-tropical climate. Summers are long and warm. Winters are short and mild. The mean annual temperature is 68.4 F. July's average is 82.3 F., while January averages 54.1 F. The average annual rainfall is 54.7 inches. Its vicinity has the lowest hurricane frequency of any port on the Atlantic or Gulf Coasts.

Fort Frederica National Monument

The Barracks

King's Magazine, Fort Frederica National Monument

Seasoned islanders readily admit that living with insects requires a certain panache. Repellents give relief from annoying mosquitos and gnats, but technique is required for defense against yellow flies. For a couple of weeks in the spring and late summer, during their swarming onslaughts, "wear a wide brim hat," advised one local authority, "and, walk slowly, gently brushing them away, rather than running, flailing, and slapping."

Meadow, north end

Catamarans, East Beach

Great blue heron

Golden Isles Marina Village

When the U.S. Coast Guard Station was opened in 1937, dedicated to "those who died on Georgia's coast," St. Simons was without its "s." Islanders were bemused that the government had changed the spelling and discarded the final letter on the cancellation stamp on island mail. While the Coast Guard and United States Post Office enacted the different spelling, the idea of their island becoming St. Simon was unanimously ignored by visitors and residents alike. Eventually, the missing letter was formally restored.

U.S. Coast Guard Station, East Beach

Sandbar, Gould's Inlet

Shrimp boats

Shrimp boats, former site of the Sea Island Yacht Club

The secret of grasping St. Simons Island is feeling. In a crowd, winsome or indifferent, or in solitude, the island bestows contentment.

Evening, East Beach

SOURCE NOTES:

1. Burnette Vanstory, *Georgia's Land of the Golden Isles* (Athens: 1956). 3.
2. R. Edwin Green, *St. Simons Island, A Summary of Its History* (Westmoreland: 1982), 5.
3. Vanstory, *Georgia's Land of the Golden Isles*, 5.
4. Barbara Hull, *St. Simons, Enchanted Island* (Atlanta: 1980), 20.
5. Margaret Davis Cate, *Our Todays and Yesterdays*, Revised Edition (Brunswick: 1930), 56.
6. Ibid., 80.
7. Ibid., 59.
8. Phinizy Spalding, *Oglethorpe in America* (Athens: 1984), 1935.
9. Ibid., 136.
10. Ibid., 138.
11. Ibid., 137.
12. Ibid., 138.
13. Ibid., 140.
14. Vanstory, *Georgia's Land of the Golden Isles*, 136.
15. Mrs. T. M. Bennett, A Guide Book of Georgia's Golden Isles (Brunswick: 1950), 2.
16. Ibid., 6.
17. Vanstory, *Georgia's Land of the Golden Isles*, 200.
18. Coastal Georgia Historical Society, *Historic Glimpses of St. Simons Island 1736-1924*, 62.

BIBLIOGRAPHY

A Peak at the Past, A History of Our Island. A Publication of the St. Simons Island Chamber of Commerce. Written by Jean S. Alexander, Leslie Falkenberg, and Burnette Vanstory.

Bennett, Mrs. T.M. *A Guide Book of Georgia's Golden Isles.* Booklet. St. Simons Island Chamber of Commerce, 1950.

Brunswick & the Golden Isles of Georgia. Glynn County demographics and other statistical data. Brunswick, Georgia: The Brunswick – Golden Isles Chamber of Commerce.

Brunswick and The Golden Isles of Georgia. Magazine of the Brunswick – Golden Isles Chamber of Commerce. Brunswick, Georgia: Brunswick – Golden Isles Chamber of Commerce and Cal Duke Advertising, 1981.

Cate, Margaret Davis. *Our Todays and Yesterdays.* Brunswick, Georgia: Glover Brothers, 1930.

____, and Orrin Sage Wightman. *Early Days of Coastal Georgia.* Fort Frederica Association, 1955.

Christ Church, Frederica – A Brief History Leaflet. St. Simons Island, Georgia: Christ Church, Frederica.

Fort Frederica National Monument. Phamphlet. United States Department of the Interior. Washington, D.C.: U.S. Government Printing Office, 1951.

Green, R. Edwin. *St. Simons Island.* Westmoreland, New York: Arner Publications, 1982.

Gibson, Count D. *Sea Islands of Georgia.* Athens, Georgia: University of Georgia Press, 1948.

Gibson, Dot Rees. *Historic St. Simons Island, Gem of the Golden Isles.* Waycross, Georgia: Dot Gibson Publications, 1975.

Hanie, Robert, James Valentine, and Kenneth Brower. *Guale, the Golden Coast of Georgia.* Friends of the Earth, Inc. New York, New York: Seabury Press, 1974.

Historic Glimpses of St. Simons Island 1736-1924. Coastal Georgia Historical Society, 1973.

Hull, Barbara. *St. Simons, Enchanted Island.* Atlanta, Georgia: Cherokee Publishing Company, 1980.

Island Living. St. Simons Island demographics and other statistical data. The St. Simons Chamber of Commerce.

The King and Prince Beach Hotel and Villas. Newsletter. Edited by Sally Glisson. March, 1986.

Lime Kiln Procedure. Paper submitted by Curtis Childs, National Parks Service. Fort Frederica National Monument.

Lovell, Caroline Couper. *The Golden Isles of Georgia.* Boston, Massachusetts: Little, Brown and Co., 1939.

Martin, Harold H. *This Happy Isle.* Sea Island, Georgia: Sea Island Company, 1978.

Moore, Francis. *A Voyage to Georgia.* Collection of the Georgia Historical Society, Vol. 1. Brunswick, Georgia: Fort Frederica Association, 1983.

Murphy, Mary Dean, Mildred Nix Huie, and Mildred Huie Wilcox. *Kelvin Grove Plantation 1736-1986.* Brunswick, Georgia: Glover Printing Co., 1986.

Museum of Coastal History Beside the Lighthouse. Leaflet distributed by the Coastal Georgia Historical Society.

St. Simons Lighthouse. Leaflet distributed by the St. Simons Island Chamber of Commerce.

Schoettle, H.E. Taylor. *A Field Guide to Jekyll Island.* Marine Extension Service, University of Georgia.

Spalding, Phinizy. *Oglethorpe in America.* Chicago, Illinois: The University of Chicago Press, 1977.

Vanstory, Burnett. *Georgia's Land of the Golden Isles.* Athens, Georgia: The University of Georgia Press, 1956.

____ .*Ghost Stores and Superstition of Old Saint Simons.* Vanstory Collection.

Waite, Mary Abbott, and Warren Mitchell. *Epworth By The Sea, The Methodist Center.* St. Simons Island, Georgia: Epworth by the Sea.

Wood, Virginia Steel, Editor. *St. Simons Island, Georgia, Brunswick and Vacinity, Description and History.* Written by William W. Hazard, 1825. Belmont, Massachusetts: Oak Hill Press, 1974.

ACKNOWLEDGEMENTS

I can't remember the first time I went to St. Simons Island. I suppose it was to go to the beach or just ride around the island with my parents. Growing up in Hazlehurst, about 90 miles inland from St. Simons, and spending the hot summer months working at my father's sawmill, I escaped to the island as often as I could. A lot of good friends lived there. I think we spent more time on the Frederica River water skiing than anywhere else. We used David Butler's dock as our own private marina. It still amazes me that we all survived intact.

I remember St. Simons as a sleepy little island where one had to wait for boats on the Intracoastal Waterway to pass under the drawbridge at the Frederica River. That drawbridge is gone now, replaced by a four lane causeway with towering bridges. The Intracoastal Waterway was rerouted via the McKay River. St. Simons Island has changed since I have know it. New houses, condominiums, beach clubs, shops, restaurants – all the things that are associated with growth – have made a difference.

But no matter how much St. Simons has changed, the more it has stayed the same. There are some intrinsic qualities about the island that seem unalterable. The lighthouse will ever guide ships in from the ocean; the tides will rise and fall with regularity; the crabbers will work the rivers and creeks; the herons and egrets will fish the banks and shallow flats; the marsh will change colors with the seasons; the live oaks will grow more majestic.

When I started on this book, I thought I knew all there was to know about St. Simons. But as I wandered the creeks and overgrown paths, I realized that there was a part of the island I had never seen. Not that you could touch it or photograph it; it was more of a feeling, an emotion – of harmony, peace, solitude, quiet and simple beauty. It is an emotion that draws you back. This emotion is what has drawn me back again and again and has caused me to do this book.

I am indebted to some very special islanders who shared the beauty of St. Simons with me. They welcomed me to the island as one of them, and showed me things only they would know.

Special thanks to A. W. Jones III and the Sea Island Company. Without their help this book would not have been possible. Larry Delaney let me use a bedroom whenever I showed up, even it if was in the middle of the night. Thanks to Marvin Long of the Sea Island Stables, Linda King of the Coastal Georgia Historical Society Museum of Coastal History, Jean S. Alexander of the St. Simons Island Chamber of Commerce, Robert Vogel of the Ft. Frederica National Monument, and Dan Buchan at Taylor's Fish Camp. Thanks also to Atlantans Gail Fore and Karen Hazelwood for copyreading.

To Glenda Cochran and Becky Holcombe I owe more than thanks. Without them this book would not exist. Glenda wrote a truly wonderful text, and Becky designed another beautiful book. They pushed me to photograph better than I had before and tried to make me keep to the production schedule. It was a pleasure to work with them again after the Cumberland Island book. I would also like to thank my family and my wife, Cater, for their support and understanding.